I0513660

KITTEN
ANT
HORSES
WOLF
TOUCAN
KOALA
HARE
RHINOCEROS
CLOWNFISH
SEAGULL
ELEPHANT
DEER
DOBERMANN DOG

SEAL
EAGLE
LEOPARD
FROG
HAMSTER
SWANS
COW
RAM
BAT-EARED FOX
SNAIL
OWL
PUMA

The «One Color Relaxation» book series is the most stress-free coloring you'd ever tried! No thoughts. No extra skills. So fun and easy to color!

Color the attractive magic DOTS with just One Color of pen, pencil or marker to get 25 amazing pictures with animals. For better results use dark colors.

Listen to the radio, your favorite music or audio-book and enjoy your internal harmony while coloring.

This is the perfect book to take on the go as it is of the letter-size format and lightweight.

Relax just with One Color!

COPYRIGHT © 2018 BY SUNLIFE DRAWING
ALL RIGHTS RESERVED
NO PART OF THIS PUBLICATION MAY BE REPRODUCED, DISTRIBUTED, OR TRANSMITTED IN ANY FORM OR BY ANY MEANS, INCLUDING PHOTOCOPYING, RECORDING, OR OTHER ELECTRONIC OR MECHANICAL METHODS, WITHOUT THE PRIOR WRITTEN PERMISSION OF THE AUTHOR, EXCEPT IN THE CASE OF BRIEF QUOTATIONS EMBODIED IN CRITICAL REVIEWS AND CERTAIN OTHER NONCOMMERCIAL USES PERMITTED BY COPYRIGHT LAW.
MAIL@SUNLIFEDRAWING.COM
WWW.SUNLIFEDRAWING.COM

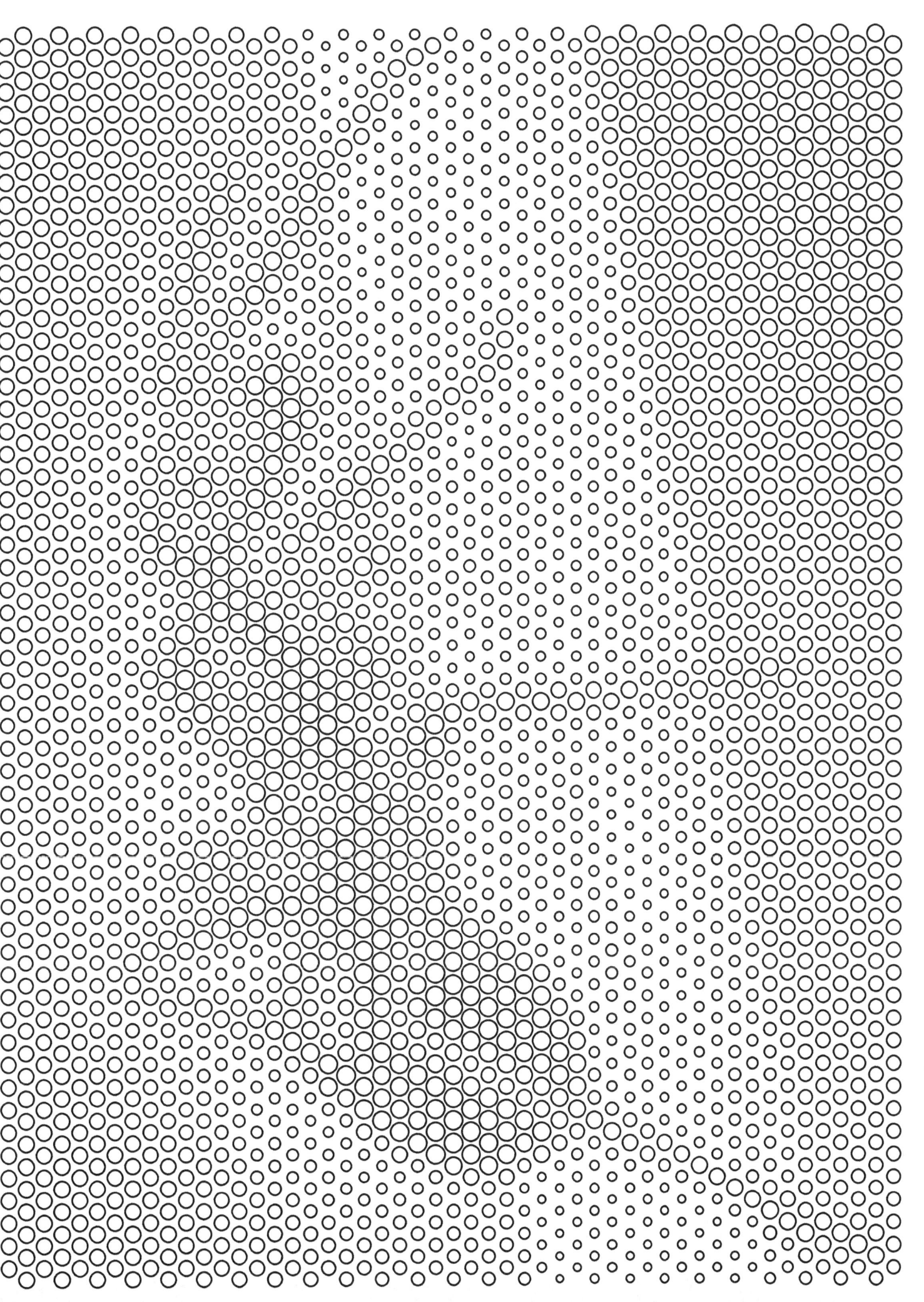

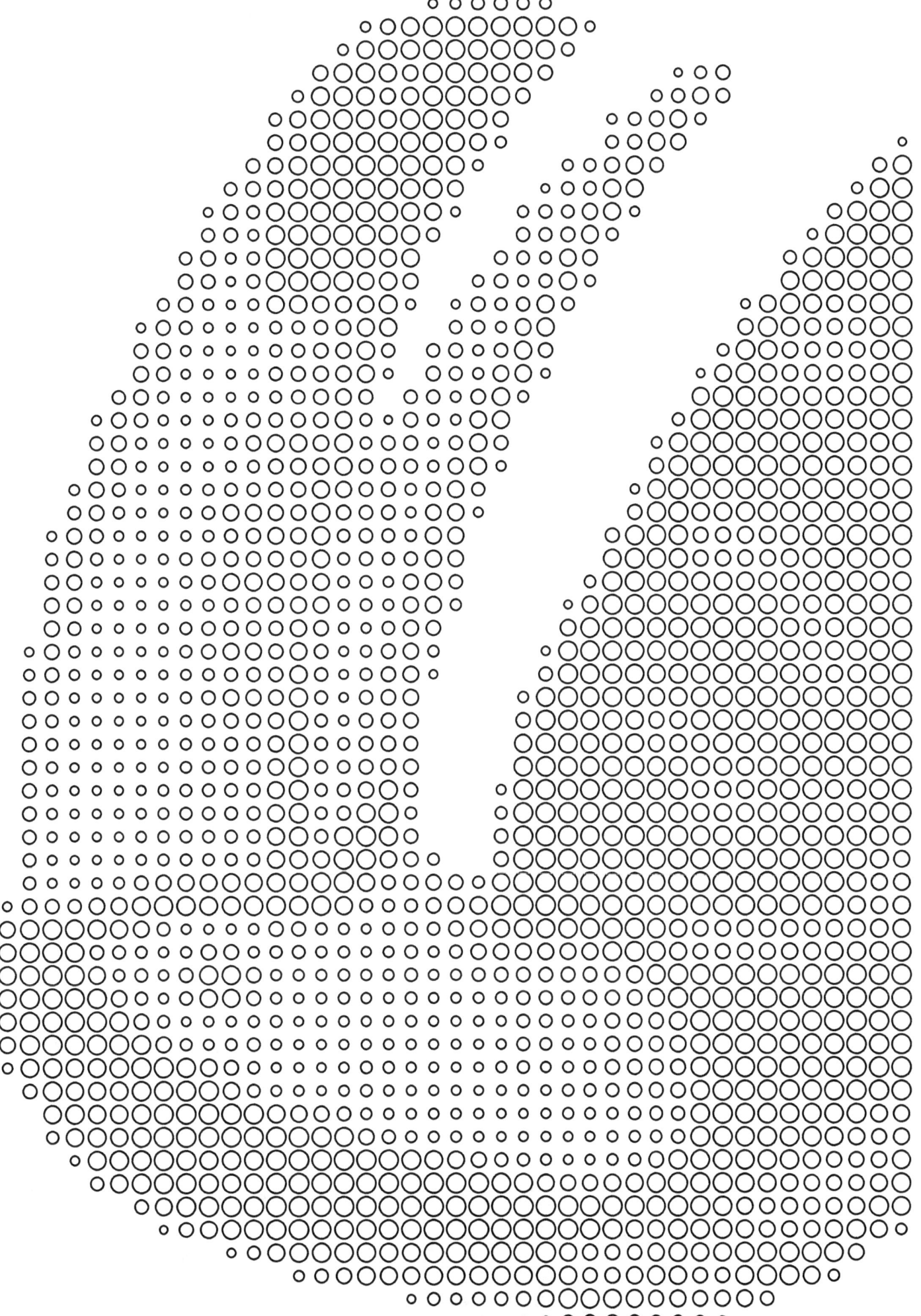

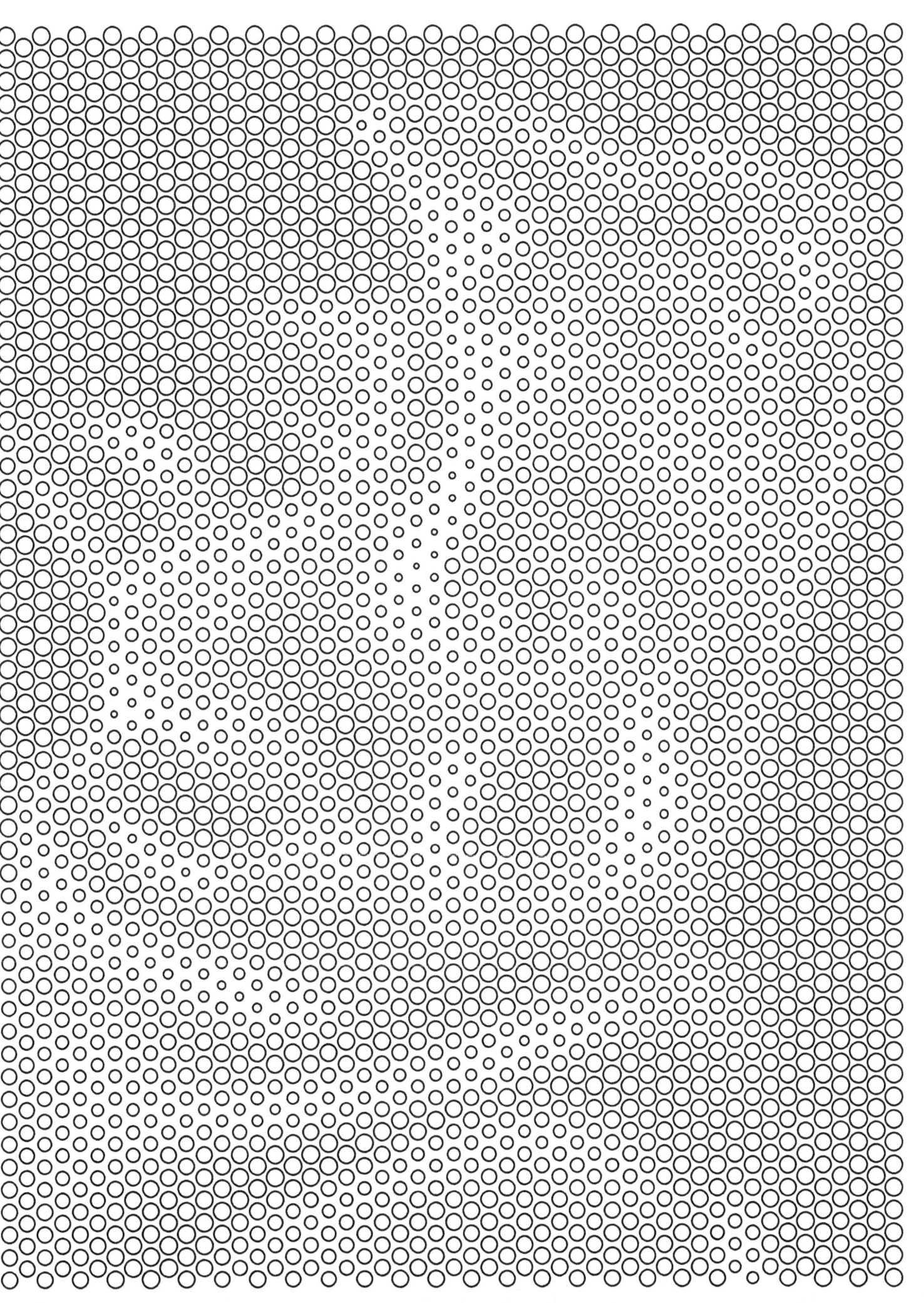

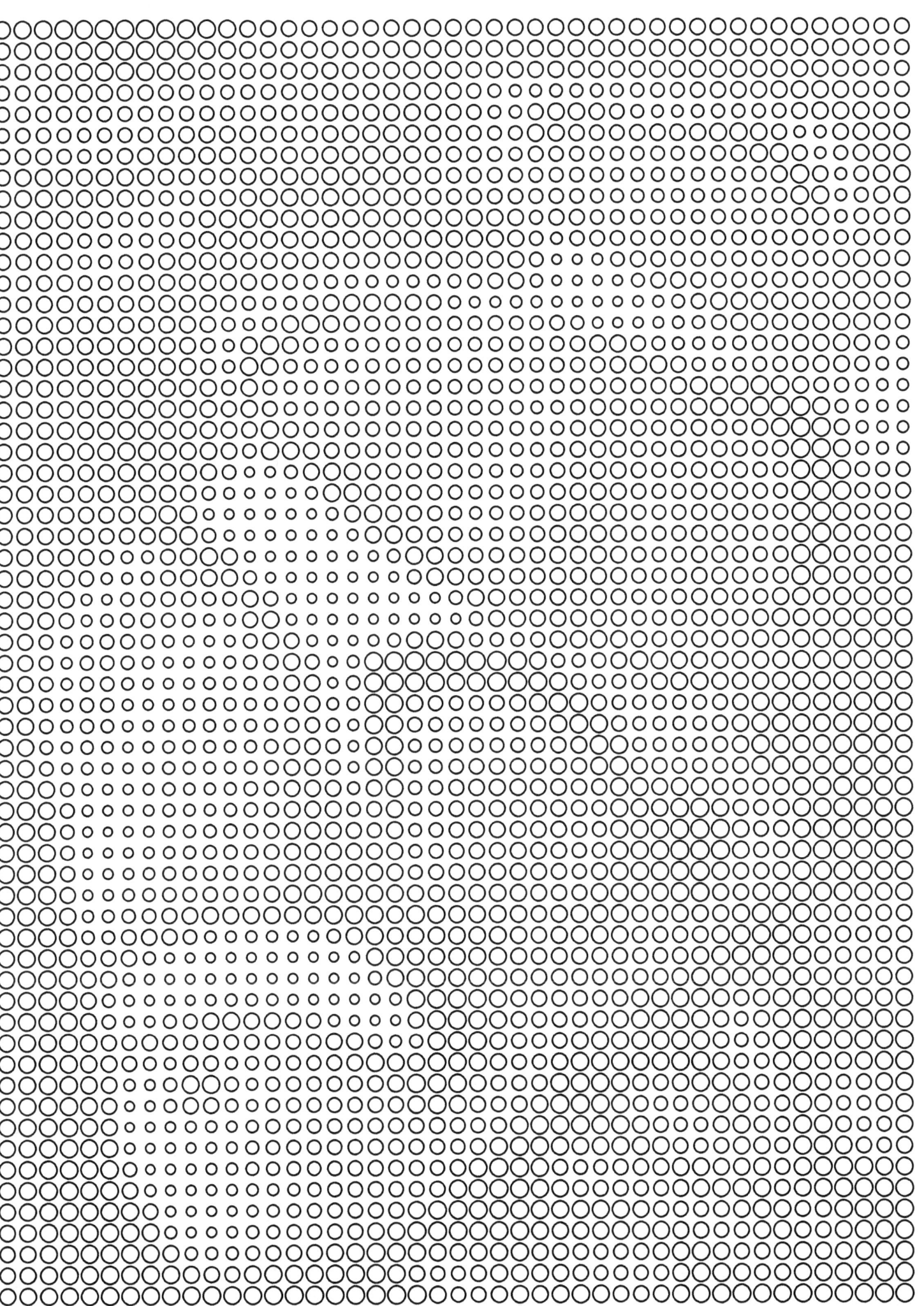

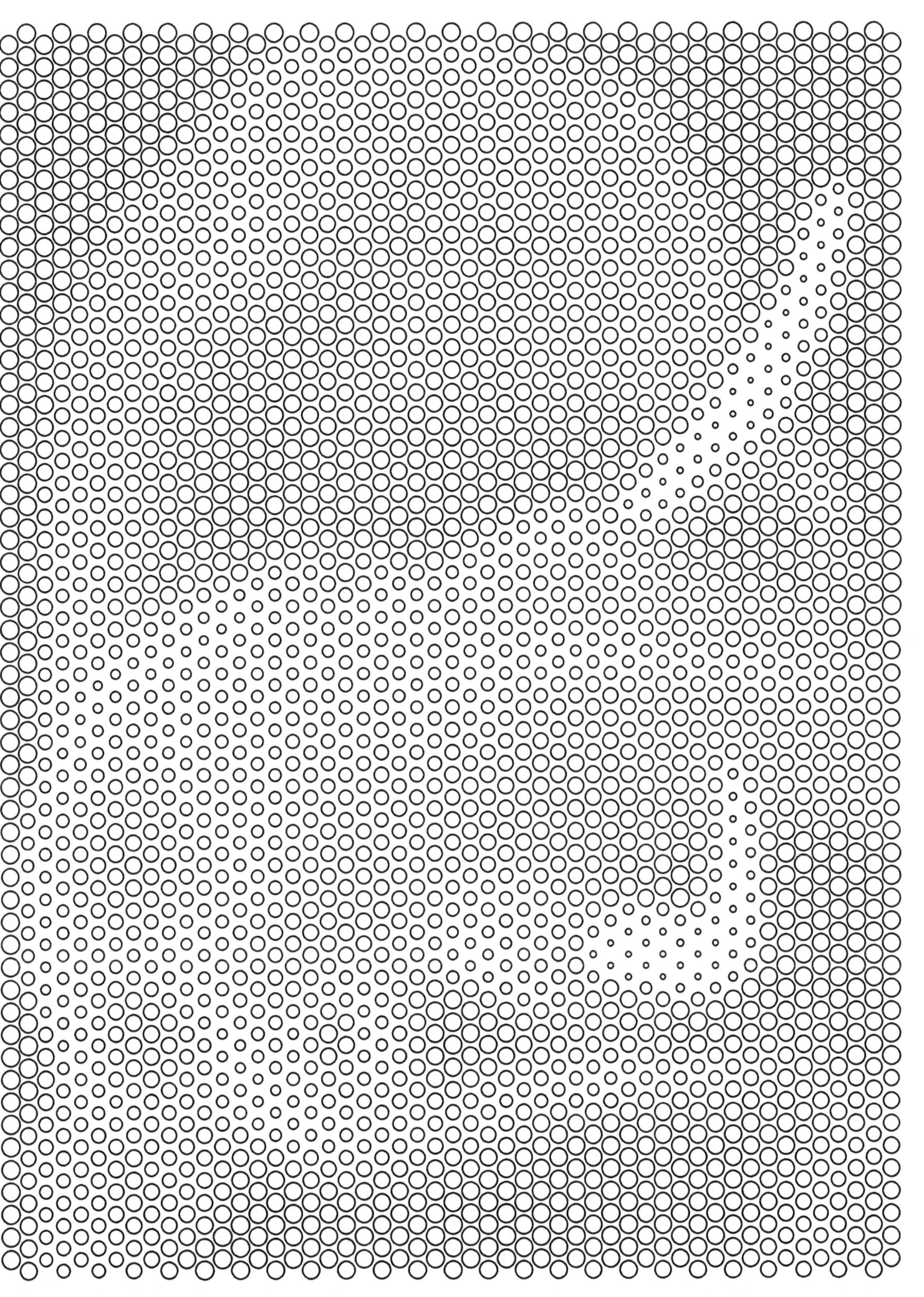

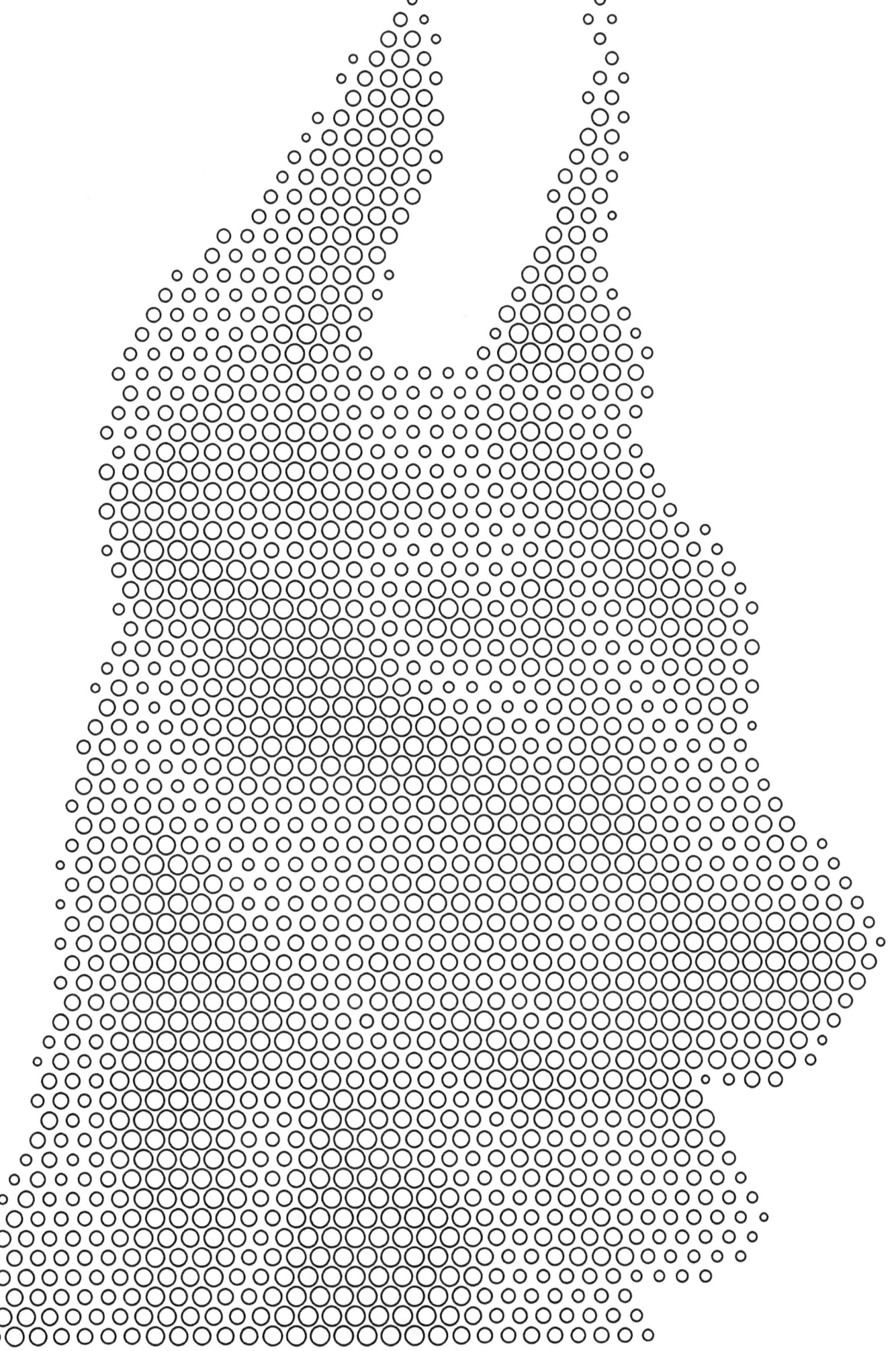

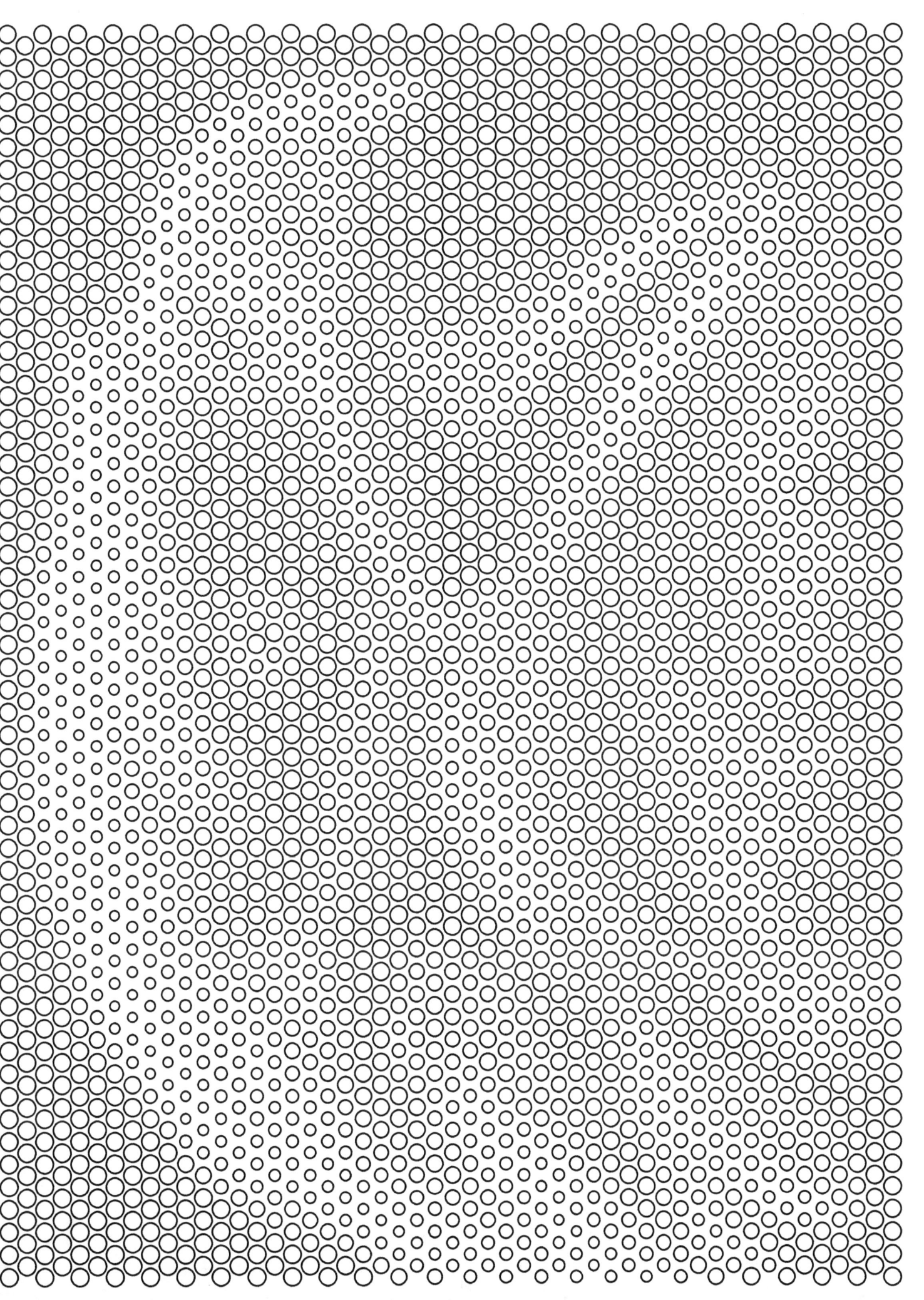

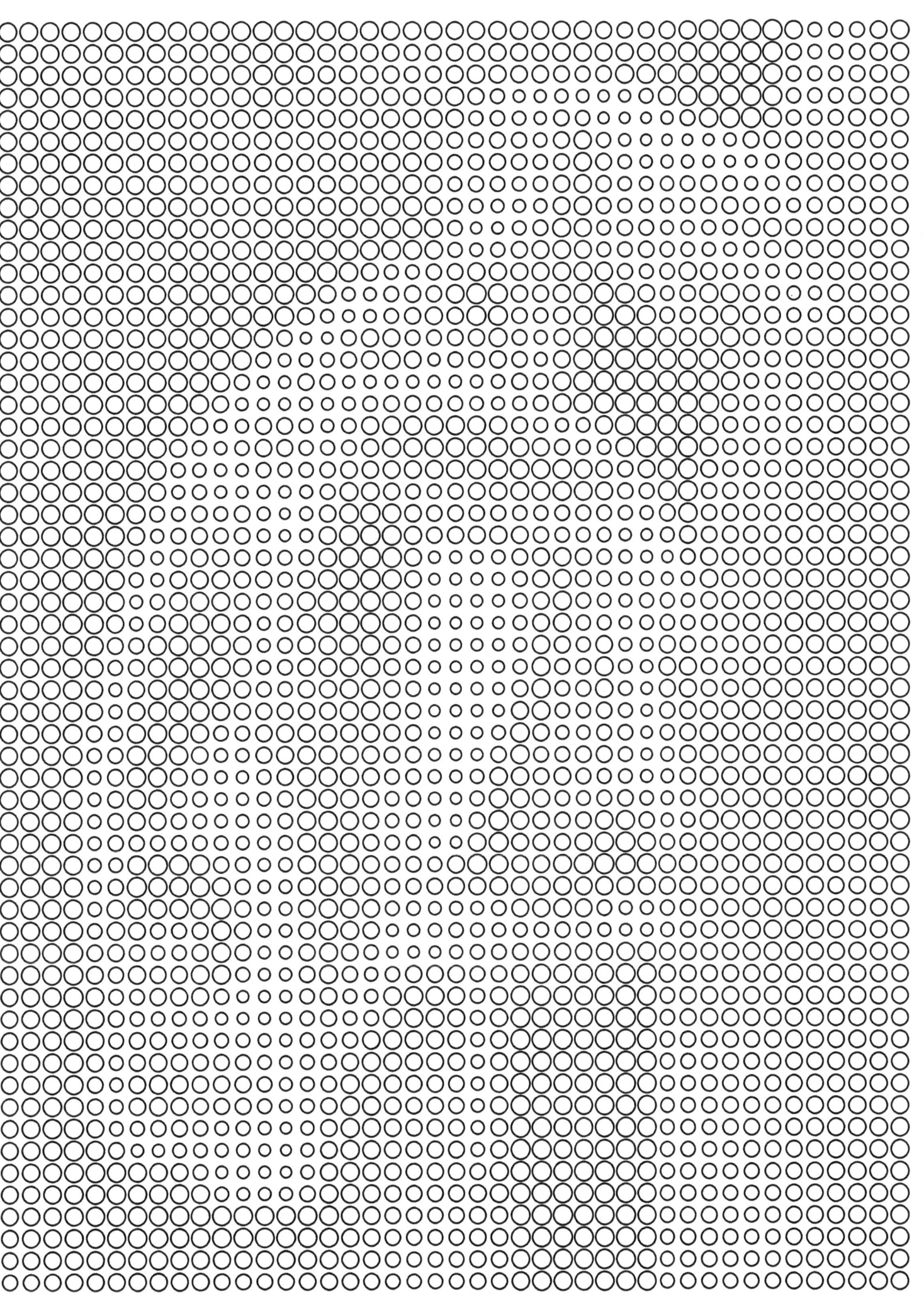

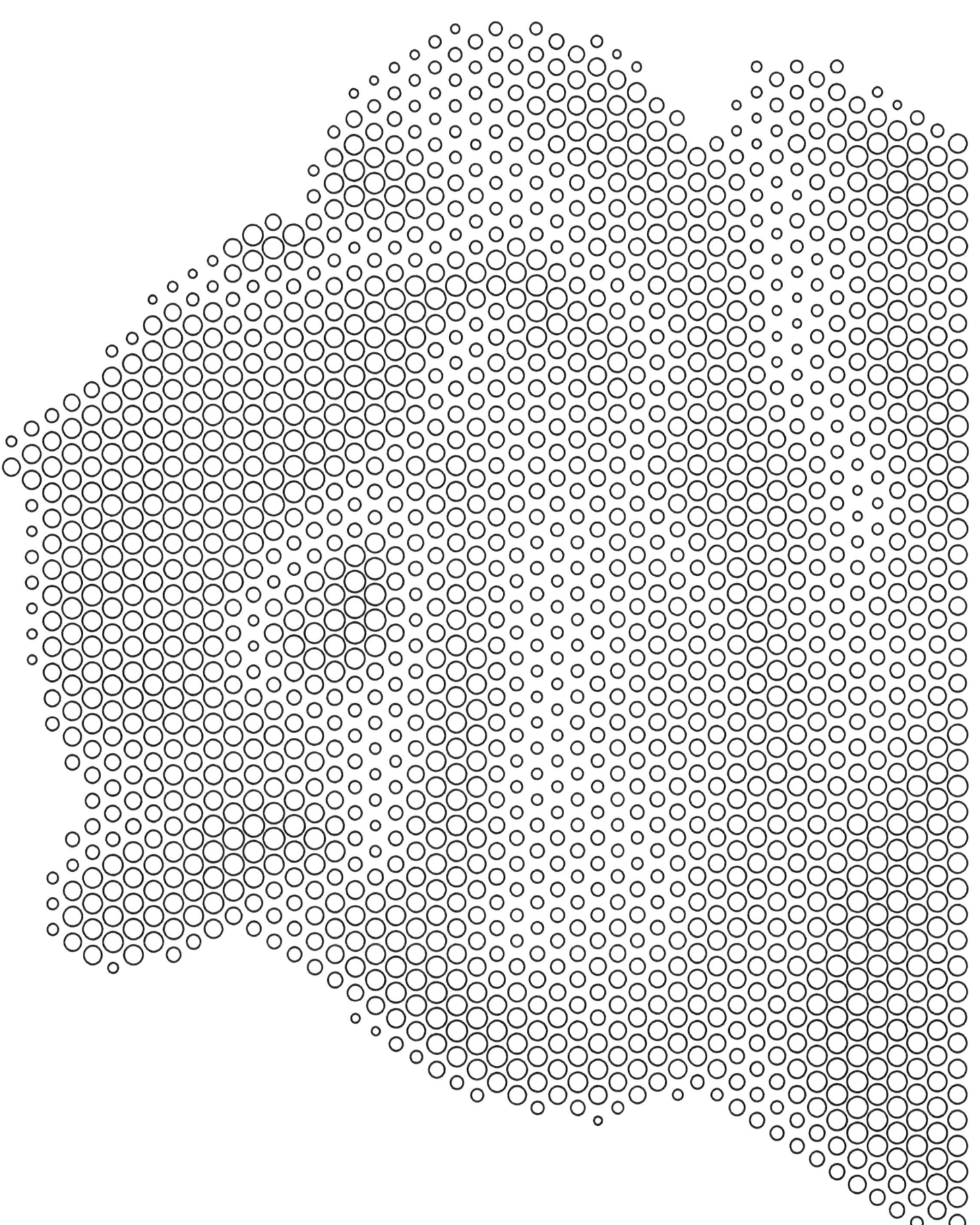

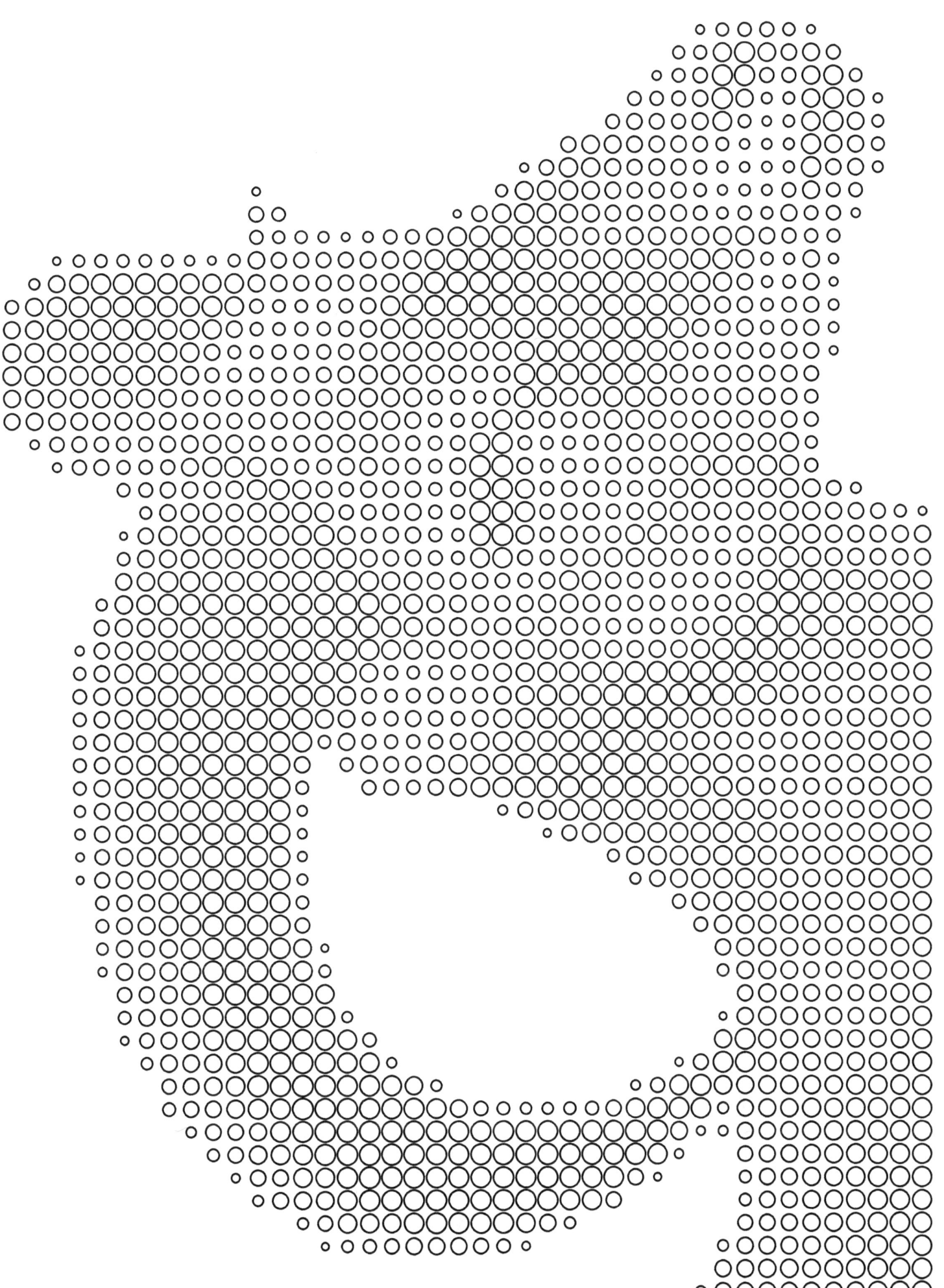

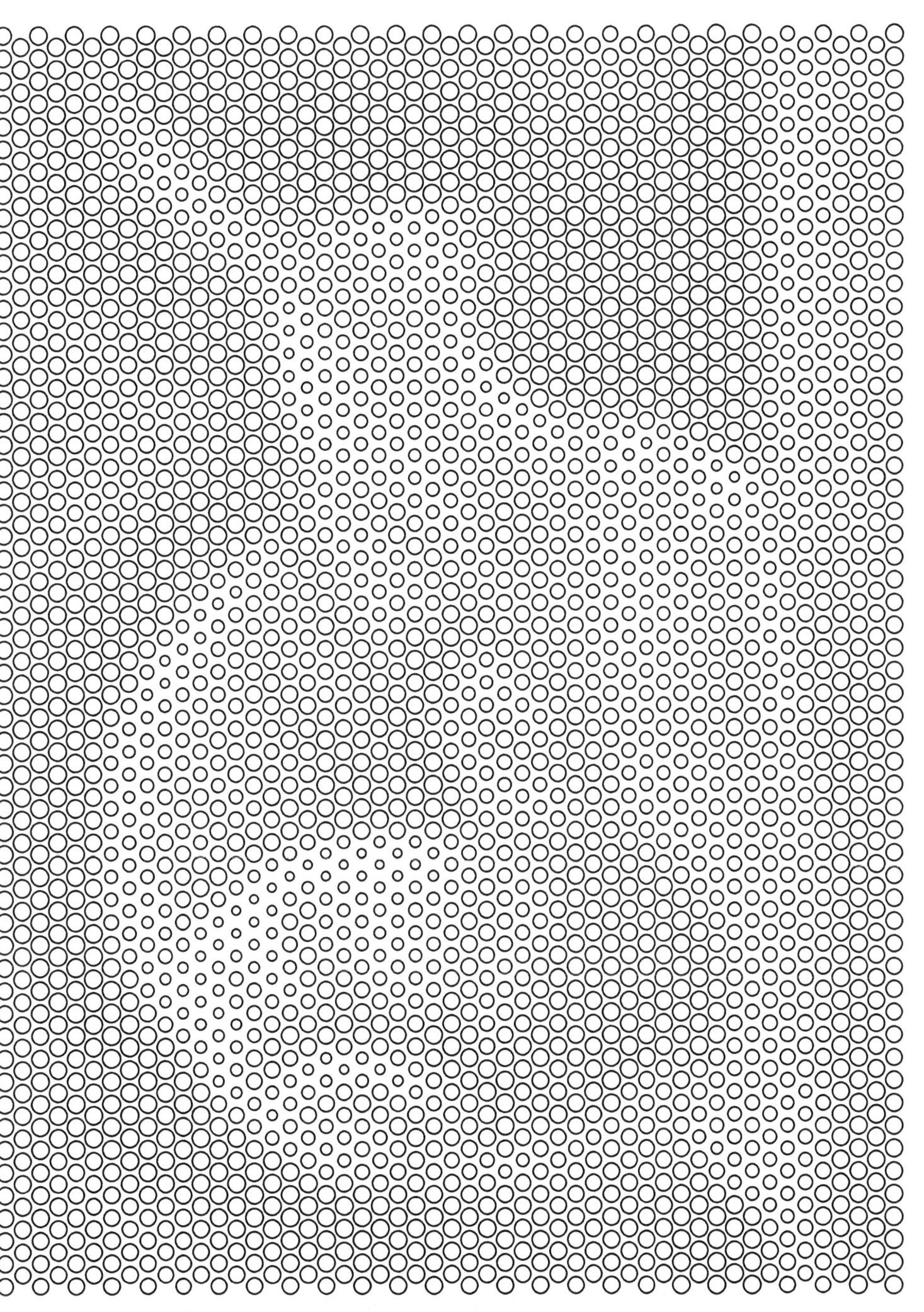

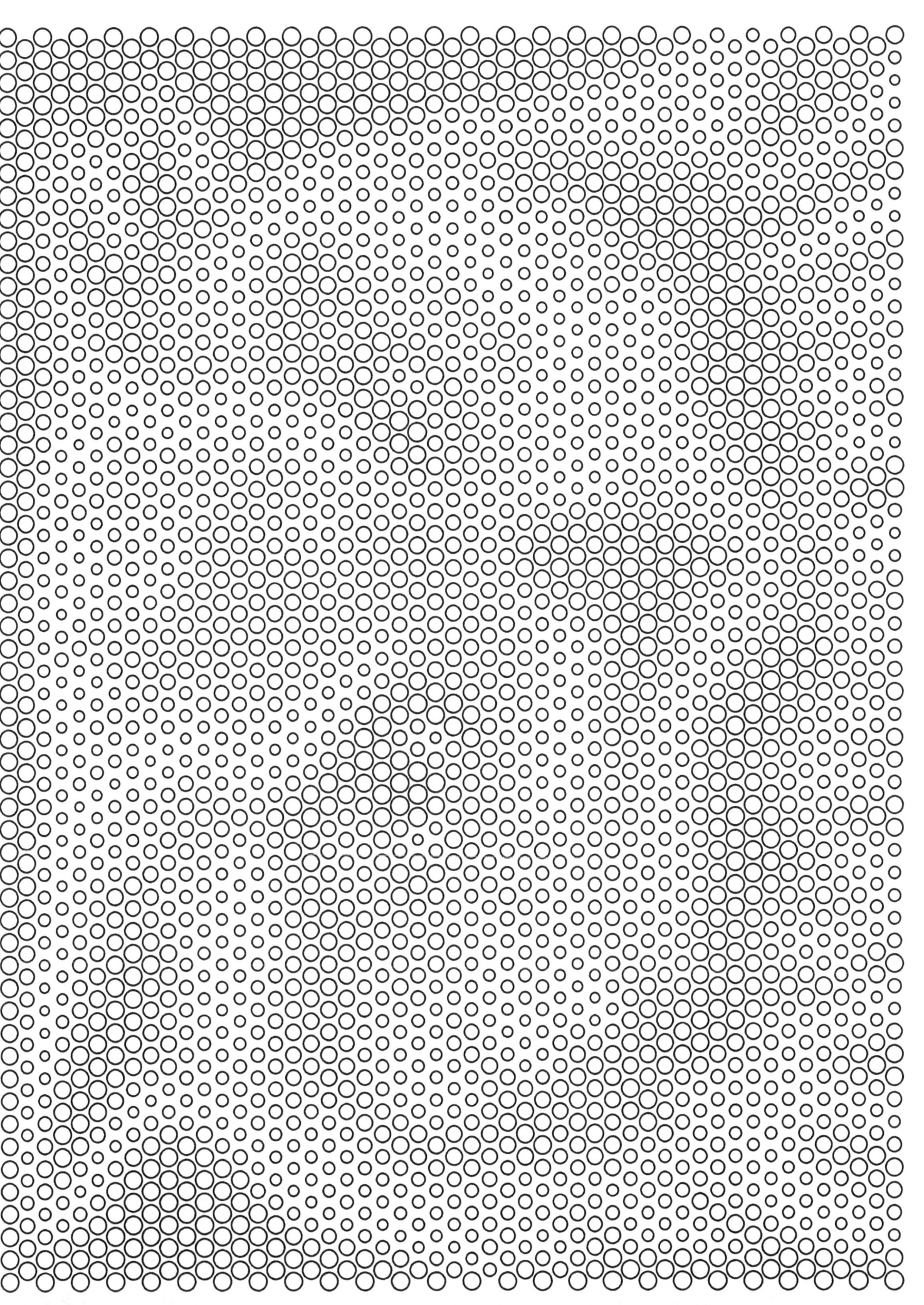

TRIAL PAGE FROM THE BOOK «ONE COLOR LINES: ANIMALS»

Thank You

for choosing this book! If you enjoyed it, please write your review on Amazon. We love hearing from our customers and your opinion is very important for us to make our books better.

Follow Us

(f) Facebook.com/SunlifeDrawing

(⊙) Instagram.com/SunlifeDrawing

www.ingramcontent.com/pod-product-compliance
Lightning Source LLC
Chambersburg PA
CBHW060005230526
45472CB00008B/1958